FIFA

WORLD CUP Guide

Gerry Cox

CARLTON

Contents

Introduction

Romario of Brazil, star of the 1994 World Cup Finals in the USA

The World Cup is the world's greatest sporting event, with an expected worldwide television audience of around 37 billion, almost double that of the 1996 Olympic Games. Every country on Earth will watch the month-long tournament unfold in France as 32 of the world's best countries compete for the title of World Champions.

South America's Brazil won the World Cup for a record fourth time four years ago in the USA, and they are favourites again this time. But hosts France will be hoping for a repeat of the last time they hosted a major tournament, when they won the European Championship in 1984, and England, Germany and Italy are also strong contenders for what is bound to be a fascinating and thrilling tournament.

A modern Norwegian Viking

It has taken 18 months of qualifying rounds to reduce the starting total of 172 countries down to the 32 who will take part in France '98. More than 600 of the world's best players will be on show, including superstars such as Ronaldo of Brazil and England's Alan Shearer.

The 64 matches will be played at 10 venues around France, with the final to decide who will become the 16th World Champions staged at the brand new Stade de France near Paris.

The French have the honour of staging the World Cup for the first time since 1938, and they have been planning for this great event for the past six years, having originally prepared a bid as far back as 1983. Four years later, in 1987, the French Football Federation gave their backing to the proposal, which was put to FIFA, football's ruling body, in 1991. A year later, FIFA ruled by 12 votes to seven to award the 16th World Cup finals to France, ahead of Morocco. Planning then began in earnest, and the draw for the qualifying stages was held in Paris back on December 12th 1995.

Two years later, when all 32 finalists were confirmed, the draw for the final stages was made in Marseille. All that was left was for the teams to prepare for the big kick-off on June 10, 1998.

The organizing committee is headed by the great Michel Platini, the best player France has ever had.

Ian Goodison of Jamaica takes to the air

Japanese fans show their colours in a qualifying game

Platini captained France during their greatest period, the early 1980s. His team have been busy making arrangements for the 2.5 million fans expected in France, improving stadiums and building the futuristic Stade de France.

During the build-up, France have created their own World Cup mascot, a cartoon cockerel called Footix, and issued commemorative coins and stamps in readiness for what will be the greatest sporting event on Earth.

Here in this invaluable guide to the World Cup finals we profile the players, the teams and the grounds which will be involved in staging this fantastic sporting show which starts in early June and ends with the final on July 12th.

Jules Rimet's Dream

The founding father – Jules Rimet (left)

It is fitting that the last World Cup of this century should be held in France because it was a Frenchman who started it all.

Jules Rimet was the man who dreamed up the idea of a tournament where the best international teams compete every four years for the title of World Champions.

It began in the 1920s, when Rimet was elected President of FIFA, the governing body of world football that was originally set up in 1904.

His plans were agreed at a meeting of FIFA in 1928 and the first tournament was held in Uruguay in 1930, with 13 teams competing, most of them from South America.

Uruguay beat Argentina 4–2 in the Final and Rimet presented the 30cm high gold trophy to their captain.

The Uruguayans did not defend their title four years later in Italy, and European teams dominated, with Italy beating Czechoslovakia 2–1 in the Final to lift the trophy for the first time.

They retained the title of World Champions four years

later in France, overcoming Brazil in the semi-finals and beating Hungary 4–2 in the exciting Final.

The Second World War prompted a 12 year absence, but the finals returned with style in 1950 and were held in Brazil. England entered for the first time but were surprisingly beaten by the USA.

Uruguay stunned over 200,000 fanatical fans in the Maracana Stadium – a World Cup record for a final – by beating hosts Brazil and lifting the trophy once again.

The 1954 finals, in Switzerland, were the highest scoring ever with 140 goals in 26 matches, and they saw a

Hungary score against Germany in the 1954 Final but lose the game

great upset when West Germany won the Final 3–2 against Hungary, who had not lost a match for four years.

Four years later in 1958, Brazil won their first title in Sweden, with an unknown 17-year-old called Pele scoring twice in the 5–2 Final win over the host country.

In 1962 the finals were staged in Chile and Pele featured again as he showed why he was rated the world's best player with some superb displays. Cruelly, injury ruled him out of Brazil's 3–1 final victory over Czechoslovakia.

Recent History

The last eight finals

Pele in action as Brazil beat Italy in 1970

1966 was the year that England, the founders of modern football, staged the finals and won at Wembley amid much controversy. England reached the Final against West Germany, who scored a late equaliser to take the game into extra time. A shot from Geoff Hurst then hit the bar and bounced down – England claimed a goal but the Germans protested that the ball had not crossed the line. A goal was awarded, though, and Hurst scored again in the closing minutes to become the only man ever to hit a hat-trick in a World Cup Final.

The Germans gained revenge four years later in Mexico, beating England in the quarter-finals, but the magnificent Brazilians beat Italy 4–1 in the Final, with Pele scoring their first goal. They were awarded the Jules Rimet Trophy for winning the competition for a third time, and a new cup was commissioned.

West Germany were the first

winners of the new cup, taking the trophy on home soil in 1974 after beating a strong Dutch side.

The hosts won in 1978, too, but this time it was Argentina, with Holland again beaten in the Final.

In Spain in 1982, Italy overcame the Germans in the Final, with Paolo Rossi their outstanding player. It meant that Italy joined Brazil as three-times winners of the tournament. They, however, did not get to keep the cup.

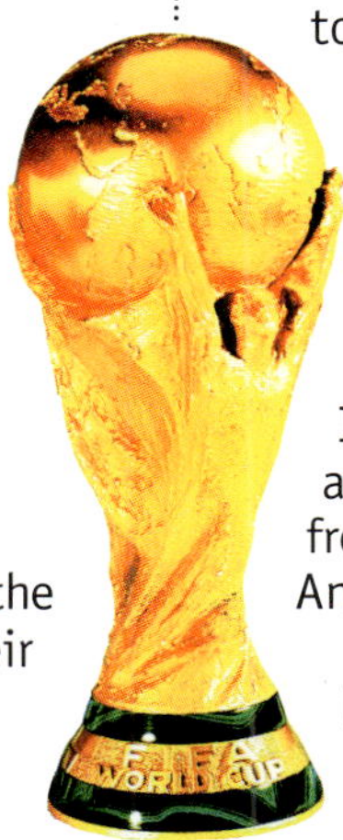

© 1974 FIFA TM

Mexico staged the tournament again in 1986, and Diego Maradona was the undoubted star as he led Argentina to victory over West Germany in the final. But revenge came four years later in Italy, when Argentina lost a poor final to a penalty from West Germany's Andreas Brehme.

1994's final in America between Brazil and Italy was just as disappointing, with no goals scored but the Brazilians claimed their fourth title on a penalty shoot-out after extra time.

Diego Maradona lifts the cup after Argentina's victory in 1986

Around the Grounds

Ten grounds in nine cities throughout France will be used during the World Cup, with the final to be staged at the brand new Stade de France.

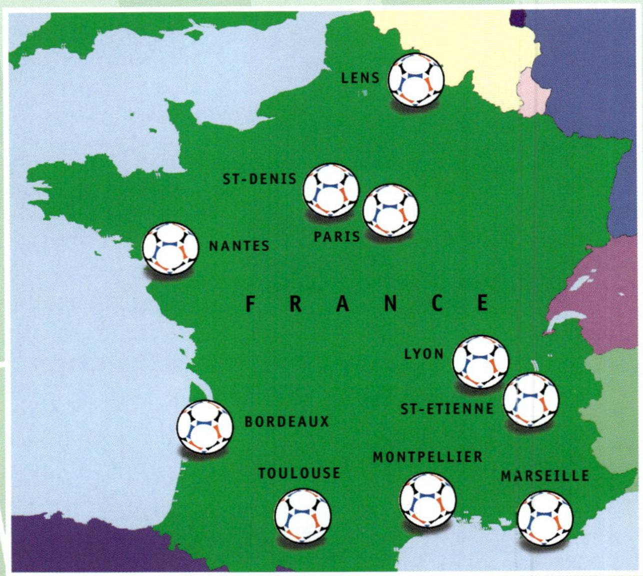

The ultra-modern Stade de France

Each city will host at least six matches, and for the first time in World Cup history each team will play their first three matches in different stadiums.

Stade de France

This state-of-the-art stadium on the outskirts of Paris has been built especially for the tournament. It will also be used for other major sporting events, concerts and shows.

Similarly, all of the other grounds have been upgraded to bring them into line with the standards required for staging such a major tournament, and France can now boast some of the best stadiums in Europe.

Bordeaux

Stade Lescure,
Place Johnston, 33000 Bordeaux

Region: Aquitaine (west France)

Home club: Girondins de Bordeaux

Stadium capacity: 36,500

Built: 1938, renovated 1986

Record attendance: 40,200
Girondins vs. Juventus, European Champions Cup 1985

Venue for: First and Second Round matches

This historical monument, home to Girondins of Bordeaux on the west coast of France, was built in the 1930s and used during the 1938 World Cup. It has since had extensive renovation work to make it an all-seater stadium with a capacity of some 36,000, of which 15,000 will be under cover.

Lens

Stade Felix Bollaert,
Rue Alfred Maès, 62300 Lens

Region: Nord Pas-de-Calais (north-east France)

Home club: Racing Club de Lens

Stadium capacity: 42,000

Built: 1934, renovated 1984

Record attendance: 45,848
Belgium vs. Yugoslavia, European Championship 1984

Venue for: First and Second Round matches

The Felix Bollaert Stadium, home to Racing Club de Lens, is near the border with Belgium in north-eastern France. It was also built during the 1930s for the 1938 World Cup, and has been converted so that it now seats just over 40,000.

Lyon

Stade de Gerland,
Avenue Jean-Jaurès, 69000 Lyon

Region: Rhône-Alpes (east France)

Home club: Olympique Lyonnais

Stadium capacity: 44,000

Built: 1926

Record attendance: 51,680
Denmark vs. Spain, European Championship 1984

Venue for: First and Second Round matches, one Quarter-Final

The grand Gerland Stadium is listed as one of France's historic monuments. It is situated in central France, and Olympique Lyonnais use it as their home ground. The capacity will remain at 44,000 but the stadium will be all-seater for the World Cup.

Marseille

Stade Vélodrome,
3 Bd. Michelet, 13008 Marseille

Region: Provence-Alpes-Côte d'Azur (south France)

Home club: Olympique de Marseille

Stadium capacity: 60,000

Built: 1937

Record attendance: 54,848
France vs. Portugal, European Championship 1984

Venue for: five Group matches, one Second Round match, a Quarter-Final and a Semi-Final

This famous stadium is in the south of France and is home to Olympique Marseille, who won the European Cup in 1993. It was first built for the 1938 World Cup and used to feature a cycling and athletics track, but has had a complete facelift and is now a 60,000 all-seater ground.

Montpellier

**Stade de la Mosson,
Avenue Heidelberg,
34000 Montpellier**

Region: Languedoc-Rousillon (south France)

Home club: Montpellier Hérault

Stadium capacity: 35,500

Built: 1988

Record attendance: 22,000 Montpellier Hérault vs. Manchester Utd, European Cup-winners Cup, 1991

Venue for: five Group matches and one Second Round match

This stadium in the south of France was only a small ground until the 1980s, when Montpellier won promotion to the First Division. It was rebuilt in 1988, and has been further upgraded for the World Cup.

Nantes

**Stade de la Beaujoire,
Route de St. Joseph, 44000 Nantes**

Region: Le Pays de Loire (north-east France)

Home club: Football Club de Nantes

Stadium capacity: 40,000

Built: 1984

Record attendance: 52,467 France vs. Belgium, European Championship 1984

Venue for: five Group matches and one Quarter-Final

Stade de la Beaujoire was built for the 1984 European Championship. It has become the second most important rugby venue in France (after Parc des Princes in Paris).

Paris

**Stade du Parc des Princes,
30 Avenue du Parc des Princes,
75016 Paris**

Region: Ile-de-France (north France)

Home club: Paris St-Germain

Stadium capacity: 49,300

Rebuilt: 1972

Record attendance: 47,000
France vs. Spain, European Championship Final 1984

Venue for: four Group matches, one Second Round match and the Third/Fourth Place play-off

Parc des Princes doubles as France's most significant rugby stadium, and was used for some of the most important matches of the 1995 Rugby World Cup. The Parc des Princes has been home to Paris St-Germain and the French national football and rugby sides since it was renovated in 1972, but will now take second place to the Stade de France in nearby St Denis.

Saint-Denis

**Stade de France,
Zac du Cornillon Nord,
93216 La Plaine, St Denis**

Region: Ile-de-France (north France)

Home club: French national side

Stadium capacity: 80,000

Built: 1997

Venue for: opening and closing ceremonies, five Group matches, one Second Round match, one Quarter-Final, one Semi-Final and the 1998 World Cup Final

This magnificent new stadium has been built especially for the World Cup and will host nine games including the final as well as the opening and closing ceremonies. The crowd capacity for football matches will be 80,000 all seated, but with the aid of moving stands, that can be increased to over 100,000 for concerts and shows, with seats installed on the pitch area.

© 1974 FIFA TM

Saint-Etienne

Stade Geoffroy-Guichard, 32 Rue Jean Snella, 42000 St Etienne

Region: Rhône-Alpes (east France)

Home club: St Etienne

Stadium capacity: 48,274

Built: 1935

Record attendance: 52,467 France vs. Yugoslavia, European Championship 1984

Venue for: First and Second Round games

Close to Lyon in the east of France, the football team St Etienne sprang to fame for their European Cup exploits in the 1970s and 80s, and their stadium earned the nickname "The Green Cauldron" because of the team's colours.

Toulouse

Stade Municipal, Allée Gabriel Biénès, 31000 Toulouse

Region: Midi-Pyrénées (south France)

Home club: Football Club de Toulouse

Stadium capacity: 37,500

Built: 1930, renovated 1984

Record attendance: 35,160 Toulouse vs. Spartak Moscow, UEFA Cup 1986

Venue for: First and Second Round games

Constructed in the 1930s for the 1938 World Cup, the Municipal Stadium is home to the football and rugby teams of Toulouse in the south-west of France. It is located on an island between the two arms of the Garonne river, and for France '98 the capacity has been increased to 37,500 seats.

The Road to France

Teams from 171 countries started out on the road to France '98, but a series of pre-qualifying games shortly after the draw was made in December 1995 reduced that total to 115. The qualifying process over the following two years finally produced 30 countries to join hosts France and holders Brazil for the greatest sporting spectacle on earth.

EUROPE

Out of 49 European countries, 14 were to join hosts France in the finals. The nine group winners qualified automatically – they were: Denmark, England, Norway, Austria, Bulgaria, Spain, Holland, Romania and Germany. They were joined by the runners-up with the best record – Scotland – while the remaining second-placed teams contested play-off games over two legs.

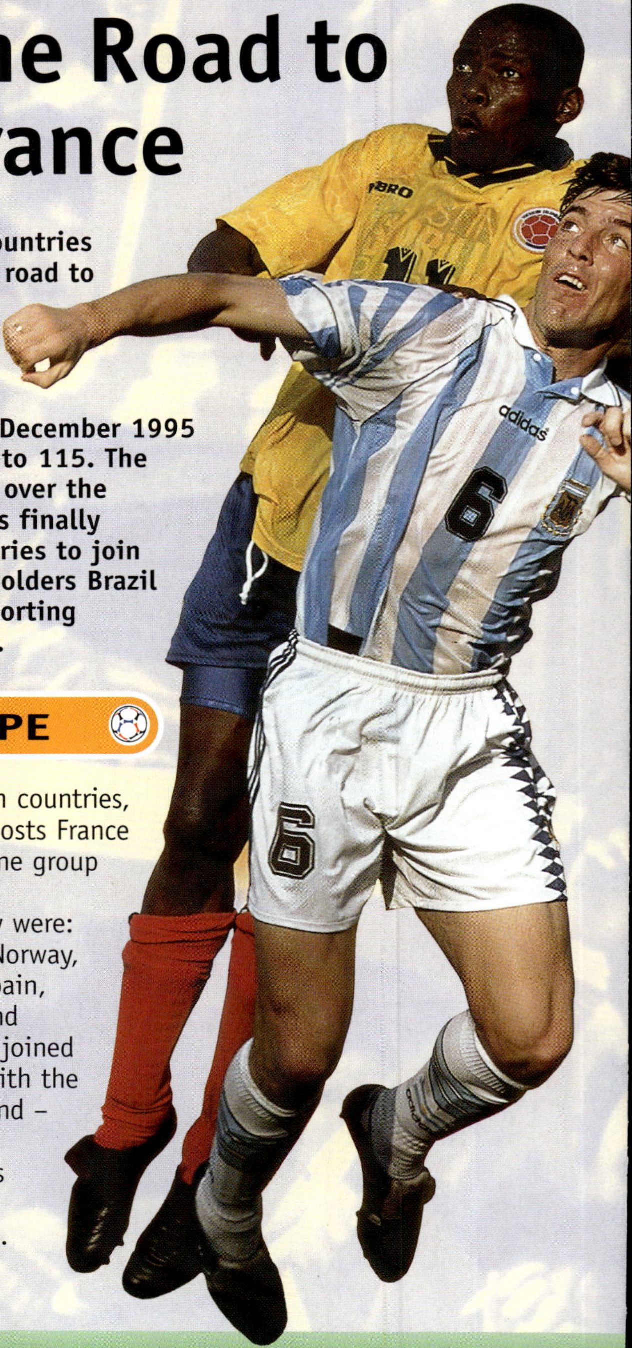

Colombia vs. Argentina

EUROPE – Group 1

Denmark finished top to qualify for the finals but it was a closely contested group. Denmark got the draw they needed in their final game in Greece, who missed out entirely as Croatia won their final match to overtake them and reach the play-offs.

TEAM	Played	Won	Drawn	Lost	For	Against	Points
Denmark	8	5	2	1	14	6	17
Croatia*	8	4	3	1	17	12	15
Greece	8	4	2	2	11	4	14
Bosnia-Herzegovina	8	3	0	5	9	14	9
Slovenia	8	0	1	7	5	20	1

* Qualified after play-off

Paul Scholes in action during England's 4–0 win over Moldova in September 1997

EUROPE – Group 2

England and Italy were pitched together in the toughest group of all, and the Italians looked favourites after winning 1–0 at Wembley. But they struggled to score goals and England grew stronger, even without their injured captain, Alan Shearer. A goalless draw in the final game in Rome meant England won the group and Italy were forced into the play-offs.

TEAM	Played	Won	Drawn	Lost	For	Against	Points
England	8	6	1	1	15	2	19
Italy*	8	5	3	0	11	1	18
Poland	8	3	1	4	10	12	10
Georgia	8	3	1	4	7	9	10
Moldova	8	0	0	8	2	21	0

* Qualified after play-off

EUROPE – Group 3

Norway won one of the weakest groups, finishing their eight games without defeat. Finland, Hungary and Switzerland all took points off each other, clearing the way for Norway to their second consecutive World Cup. Hungary reached the play-offs but were soundly beaten 12–1 on aggregate by Yugoslavia.

Norway's Egil Ostenstad takes on a couple of Swiss defenders in their qualifying game in Switzerland

TEAM	Played	Won	Drawn	Lost	For	Against	Points
Norway	8	6	2	0	21	2	20
Hungary	8	3	3	2	10	8	12
Finland	8	3	2	3	11	12	11
Switzerland	8	3	1	4	11	12	10
Azerbaijan	8	1	0	7	3	22	3

EUROPE – Group 4

Austria won the group but Scotland also qualified as the runners-up with the best record. It was a close-fought battle between those two countries and Sweden, who finished third in the 1994 finals but missed out this time. Austria's excellent home form carried them through, while Scotland's tough defence saw them let in only three goals in 10 games.

TEAM	Played	Won	Drawn	Lost	For	Against	Points
Austria	10	8	1	1	17	4	25
Scotland	10	7	2	1	15	3	23
Sweden	10	7	0	3	16	9	21
Latvia	10	3	1	6	10	14	10
Estonia	10	1	1	8	4	16	4
Belarus	10	1	1	8	5	21	4

EUROPE – Group 5

Bulgaria, who finished fourth in the 1994 finals, won the group but only after a shock defeat by Israel in their first game. They recovered to win six games in a row including a 1–0 victory over their main rivals Russia, who were forced into a play-off against Italy, which they lost over two legs.

TEAM	Played	Won	Drawn	Lost	For	Against	Points
Bulgaria	8	6	0	2	18	9	18
Russia	8	5	2	1	19	5	17
Israel	8	4	1	3	9	7	13
Cyprus	8	3	1	4	10	15	10
Luxembourg	8	0	0	8	2	22	0

EUROPE – Group 6

Spain's goalie Andoni Zubizarreta

Spain finished top without losing a match to reach their fifth consecutive finals. Yugoslavia finished second to make the play-offs but there was no place for the Czech Republic, who were runners-up in the European Championship only a year earlier.

TEAM	Played	Won	Drawn	Lost	For	Against	Points
Spain	10	8	2	0	26	6	26
Yugoslavia*	10	7	2	1	29	7	23
Czech Republic	10	5	1	4	16	6	16
Slovakia	10	5	1	4	18	14	16
Faroe Islands	10	2	0	8	10	31	6
Malta	10	0	0	10	2	37	0

* Qualified after play-off

EUROPE – Group 7

Holland's Aron Winter eludes a Belgian defender

Holland won their group in convincing fashion as they beat their main rivals Belgium both home and away and also thrashed Wales 7–1. Their only defeat came in Turkey. Belgium made sure of a play-off place ahead of Turkey by beating Wales in their final match. They went on to beat the Republic of Ireland and claim one of the last places at France '98.

TEAM	Played	Won	Drawn	Lost	For	Against	Points
Holland	8	6	1	1	26	4	19
Belgium*	8	6	0	2	20	11	18
Turkey	8	4	2	2	21	9	14
Wales	8	2	1	5	20	21	7
San Marino	8	0	0	8	0	42	0

* Qualified after play-off

EUROPE – Group 8

Romania recovered from their early exit in Euro 96 to reach France with two games to spare. They won their first nine qualifiers with ease but spoiled their perfect record by drawing their final game in Ireland, who reached a play-off with Belgium.

TEAM	Played	Won	Drawn	Lost	For	Against	Points
Romania	10	9	1	0	37	4	28
Republic of Ireland	10	5	3	2	22	8	18
Lithuania	10	5	2	3	11	8	17
FYR Macedonia	10	4	1	5	22	18	13
Iceland	10	2	3	5	11	16	9
Liechtenstein	10	0	0	10	3	52	0

EUROPE – Group 9

Germany, in a tough group with the Ukraine and Portugal, kept up their record of reaching every World Cup finals since 1954. But they struggled in their final game against bottom club Albania, who were leading before finally losing 4–3, a result that put the Ukrainians into the play-offs ahead of Portugal.

Oliver Bierhoff helped Germany qualify for their twelfth successive finals

TEAM	Played	Won	Drawn	Lost	For	Against	Points
Germany	10	6	4	0	23	9	22
Ukraine	10	6	2	2	10	6	20
Portugal	10	5	4	1	12	4	19
Armenia	10	1	5	4	8	17	8
Northern Ireland	10	1	4	5	6	10	7
Albania	10	1	1	8	7	20	4

EUROPEAN Play-offs

The strongest countries triumphed. Italy beat Russia at home after an away draw, while Yugoslavia racked up a 12–1 aggregate (total score after both matches) win over Hungary. Ireland lost to Belgium, who won 2–1 after a 1–1 draw in Dublin, while Croatia beat Ukraine 3–1 on aggregate to reach the finals for the first time.

Aggregate Scores

Italy	2–1	Russia
Belgium	12–1	Hungary
Yugoslavia	3–2	Republic of Ireland
Croatia	3–1	Ukraine

SOUTH AMERICA

For the first time, nine South American countries played in one group to decide the four qualifiers to join holders Brazil in the finals. Paraguay and Colombia made the early running and were the first to qualify but Argentina struggled at first before making good. Chile won the final place to reach the finals for the first time in 16 years.

TEAM	Played	Won	Drawn	Lost	For	Against	Points
Argentina	16	8	6	2	23	13	30
Paraguay	16	9	2	5	21	14	29
Colombia	16	8	4	4	23	15	28
Chile	16	7	4	5	32	18	25
Peru	16	7	4	5	19	20	25
Ecuador	16	6	3	7	22	21	21
Uruguay	16	6	3	7	18	21	21
Bolivia	16	4	5	7	18	21	17
Venezuela	16	0	3	13	8	41	3

CONCACAF

North and Central America were allocated three places from a final group of six who had all played pre-qualifying games. Mexico were clear favourites and won the group comfortably, with USA second and Jamaica causing the biggest surprise by qualifying for the first time.

Jamaica's Peter Cargill on the ball

TEAM	Played	Won	Drawn	Lost	For	Against	Points
Mexico	10	4	6	0	23	7	18
United States	10	4	5	1	17	9	17
Jamaica	10	3	5	2	17	12	14
Costa Rica	10	3	3	4	13	12	12
El Salvador	10	2	4	4	11	16	10
Canada	10	1	3	6	5	20	6

ASIA

South Korea qualified for their fourth successive finals by winning their second round group, as did Saudi Arabia, who played previously in 1994. The second-placed teams in each group – Japan and Iran – contested a play-off which was won by Japan, who became the first ever nation to qualify for a World Cup with a golden goal. Iran earned a play-off place against Australia.

ASIA – Group A

TEAM	Played	Won	Drawn	Lost	For	Against	Points
Saudi Arabia	8	4	2	2	8	6	14
Iran*	8	3	3	2	13	8	12
China	8	3	2	3	11	14	11
Qatar	8	3	1	4	7	10	10
Kuwait	8	2	2	4	7	8	8

* Qualified after play-off

ASIA – Group B

TEAM	Played	Won	Drawn	Lost	For	Against	Points
South Korea	8	6	1	1	19	7	19
Japan*	8	3	4	1	17	9	13
United Arab Emirates	8	2	3	3	9	12	9
Uzbekistan	8	1	3	4	13	18	6
Kazakhstan	8	1	3	4	7	19	6

* Qualified after play-off

ASIA-OCEANIA Play-off

Asia's play-off losers, Iran, met Australia, the winners of the Oceania section, to decide who would fill the last place at France '98. After a 1–1 draw at home, Iran's 2–2 result in Melbourne meant they won through on away goals.

AFRICA

Five African countries qualified for the finals for the first time, bringing yet more international flavour to the World Cup Finals.

AFRICA – Group 1

Nigeria reached their second successive finals by winning a tight group from Guinea, who beat them in the final game but lost out by one point. The Green Eagles are a strong side and great things are expected of them.

TEAM	Played	Won	Drawn	Lost	For	Against	Points
Nigeria	6	4	1	1	10	4	13
Guinea	6	4	0	2	10	5	12
Kenya	6	3	1	2	11	12	10
Burkina Faso	6	0	0	6	7	17	0

AFRICA – Group 2

Tunisia surprised many people by winning the group comfortably ahead of Egypt, traditionally one of Africa's strongest football countries. A 1–0 defeat in Tunisia and a goalless draw at home sealed the fate of the Egyptians and saw Tunisia through to the finals for only the second time.

TEAM	Played	Won	Drawn	Lost	For	Against	Points
Tunisia	6	5	1	0	10	1	16
Egypt	6	3	1	2	15	5	10
Liberia	6	1	1	4	2	10	4
Namibia	6	1	1	4	6	17	4

AFRICA – Group 3

South Africa, the reigning African Nations Champions, won their group ahead of Congo, who had beaten them 2–0 in an early game. But South Africa won the return game and Congo's defeat by Zambia meant they missed out.

TEAM	*Played*	*Won*	*Drawn*	*Lost*	*For*	*Against*	*Points*
South Africa	6	4	1	1	7	3	13
Congo	6	3	1	2	5	5	10
Zambia	6	2	2	2	7	6	8
Congo DR	6	0	2	4	4	9	2

AFRICA – Group 4

The Indomitable Lions of Cameroon qualified for their third successive finals by finishing ahead of Angola without losing a game.

TEAM	*Played*	*Won*	*Drawn*	*Lost*	*For*	*Against*	*Points*
Cameroon	6	4	2	0	10	4	14
Angola	6	2	4	0	7	4	10
Zimbabwe	6	1	1	4	6	7	4
Togo	6	1	1	4	6	14	4

AFRICA – Group 5

Morocco, another of Africa's football superpowers, won their group by a big margin of nine points from second-placed Sierra Leone, and were unbeaten throughout.

TEAM	*Played*	*Won*	*Drawn*	*Lost*	*For*	*Against*	*Points*
Morocco	6	5	1	0	14	2	16
Sierra Leone	5	2	1	2	4	6	7
Ghana	6	1	3	2	7	7	6
Gabon	5	0	1	4	1	11	1

Brazil

Group A

Ronaldo, Roberto Carlos and co. celebrate at Le Tournoi

Founded: 1914

FIFA: 1923

Regarded by many as the greatest footballing nation in the world, Brazil have won the World Cup a record four times and are current World Champions. Their first success was in 1958 with a 17-year-old Pele, who went on to become the greatest player in the history of football. Now they have Ronaldo, Rivaldo and Denilson, the three most expensive players in the world and are once again coached by Mario Zagallo, who won the World Cup twice as a player and in 1970 as coach.

Previous best in World Cup: Winners 1958, 1962, 1970, 1994

Other honours: Copa America champions four times

Coach: Mario Zagallo

Star players: Ronaldo, Rivaldo, Roberto Carlos

Past masters: Pele, Zico, Socrates

Scotland

Group A

Scotland qualify for the World Cup finals with a 2–0 win over Latvia

Founded: 1873

FIFA: 1910–1920, 1924–1928, 1946

Craig Brown is hoping to lead Scotland further than the first round in their eighth appearance in the World Cup finals. Scotland have always been capable in qualifying for the World Cup, but once there have failed to impress, losing to the likes of Peru and Costa Rica in the past and being held by Iran. They don't have outstanding individuals but are solid with a tight defence and will be difficult to beat.

Previous best in World Cup: Never gone beyond first round.

Other honours: European Championships – First round in 1992 and 1996

Coach: Craig Brown

Star players: Colin Hendry, Kevin Gallacher, Gary McAllister

Past masters: Kenny Dalglish, Graeme Souness, Denis Law

Morocco

Group A

Founded: 1955

FIFA: 1956

This is Morocco's fourth appearance in the finals, although they have only reached the second round once, in 1986. This time they have the benefit of former French national coach Henri Michel, who took France to third place in the 1986 World Cup and led Cameroon to USA '94. His strong Moroccan side won their qualifying group by the huge margin of nine points and were unbeaten.

Nourredine Naybet tangles with Kim Tyrone from Ghana

Previous best in World Cup: Reached second round in 1986

Other honours: African Nations Cup winners in 1976

Coach: Henri Michel

Star players: Sala Bassir, Nourredine Naybet, Said Chiba

Past masters: Larbi Ben Barek, Mohammed Timmoumi, Aziz Bouderbala

Norway

Group A

Roger Nilsen and Ronny Johnsen celebrate winning against Switzerland

Founded: 1902

FIFA: 1908

Norway are hoping to go further than in their previous two tournaments, when they were knocked out in the first round. They have become a rising power in European football under coach Egil Olsen, who plays a well-organised and direct style. The standard of Norwegian football has progressed a lot over the past 10 years and many players are now with top clubs in England and other European countries.

Previous best in World Cup: Knocked out in first round 1938 and 1994

Other honours: None

Coach: Egil Olsen

Star players: Tore Andre Flo, Oyvind Leonhardsen, Henning Berg

Past masters: Erik Thorstvedt, Jostein Flo, Kjetil Rekdal

Italy

Group B

Italy qualified after having to beat Russia in a play-off

Founded: 1898

FIFA: 1903

Italy beat Russia in the play-offs after finishing second to England in the qualifying rounds, having struggled to score goals. But they will still be among the favourites in France because of their track record in the World Cup, having won it three times and reached the final twice more, the most recent being at USA '94. Cesare Maldini has a talented squad that should reach the final stages of France '98.

Previous best in World Cup: Winners 1934, 1938, 1982

Other honours: European Champions 1968, Olympic Champions 1936

Coach: Cesare Maldini

Star players: Paolo Maldini, Gianfranco Zola, Alessandro Del Piero

Past masters: Roberto Baggio, Paolo Rossi, Luigi Riva

Chile

Group B

Founded: 1895

FIFA: 1912

Chile have now qualified seven times for the finals of the World Cup, but apart from their third place in 1962 when they were hosts, they have failed to progress past the first round. They were the last team to qualify from the South American group and are not expected

Chile will be going to France hoping to improve on their finals' record

to progress too far, but they have two quality strikers in Ivan Zamorano and Marcelo Salas.

Previous best in World Cup: Finished third in 1962

Other honours: Copa America runners-up 1979 and 1987

Coach: Nelson Acosta

Star players: Marcello Salas, Ivan Zamorano

Past masters: Leonel Sanchez, Carlos Caszely, Eladio Rojas

Cameroon

Group B

Cameroon celebrate a goal

Founded: 1960

FIFA: 1962

Cameroon, known as "The Indomitable Lions", surprised everyone at Italia '90 by beating World Cup holders Argentina in the opening game and then reaching the quarter-finals before losing to England in extra time. Then they were inspired by Roger Milla, one of the greatest players in the history of African football. They are coached by former international Jean Manga Onguene, who hopes to go better than the first round knockouts of 1982 and 1994.

Previous best in World Cup: Reached quarter-finals in 1990

Other honours: African Nations Cup winners in 1984 and 1988, runners-up in 1986

Coach: Jean Manga Onguene

Star players: Jacques Songo'o, Rigobert Song, Marc-Vivien Foe

Past masters: Roger Milla, Omam Biyik, Joseph Antoine-Bell

Austria

Group B

The Austrian team were overjoyed when they qualified

Founded: 1904

FIFA: 1905

This is Austria's seventh visit to the World Cup finals but they have not had any success since the early years. Austria were a great football power in the 1920s and 30s, and reached the semi-finals in 1934 and 1954, winning the third-place play-off that year. Recent participation has been less successful, but the appointment of Herbert Prohaska has captured the imagination of the footballing public.

Previous best in World Cup: 3rd place in 1954

Other honours: European Championship last 8 in 1960

Coach: Herbert Prohaska

Star players: Toni Polster, Andreas Herzog, Michael Konsel

Past masters: Ernst Happl, Hans Krankl, Franz Binder

France

Group C

Founded: 1918

FIFA: 1904

France are bound to be among the favourites because they are hosts, but their form in the build-up has not been too encouraging. Although they were founding members of FIFA and launched the first World Cup, the only time they were a footballing world power was in the 1980s, when they reached two World Cup semi-finals, won the European Championship and the Olympics in a four-year spell, with stars such as Michel Platini, Jean Tigana and Alain Giresse.

Previous best in World Cup: 3rd place in 1986

Other honours: European Championship winners in 1984, Olympic winners 1984

Coach: Aimé Jacquet

Star players: Youri Djorkaeff, Didier Deschamps, Zinecine Zidane

Past masters: Just Fontaine, Michel Platini, Jean-Pierre Papin

South Africa

Group C

South Africa's David Nyathi in action

Founded: 1892

FIFA: 1952 (suspended 1964–76), 1992

South Africa have only recently emerged as a force in African football after they rejoined FIFA in 1992 following a long absence for political reasons. Since then, before leaving, coach Clive Barker built a strong side which won the African Nations Cup by beating Tunisia 2–0 in Johannesburg in 1996, and they qualified for their first World Cup finals soon afterward. Their success has led to many players moving to strong European countries such as Italy and England.

Previous best in World Cup: First appearance

Other honours: African Nations Cup winners in 1996

Coach: Philippe Troussier

Star players: Mark Fish, Lucas Radebe, Phil Masinga

Saudi Arabia

Group C

In early November, 1997 the Saudi Arabian team celebrated after their 2–0 victory over Qatar which guaranteed them a place in France

Founded: 1959

FIFA: 1959

An impressive performance in their first World Cup in 1994, where they finished second in their group after beating Belgium and Morocco, proved that the Saudi Arabians had emerged as a force in Asian football. They again look strong after winning their Asian qualifying group by overtaking Iran in the final stages. The team are under the charge of their third coach in a year – Carlos Parreira took over from Otto Pfister in late 1997.

Previous best in World Cup: Last 16 in 1994

Other honours: Asian Cup winners 1984 and 1988

Coach: Carlos Alberto Parreira

Star players: Khaled Musaad, Mohammed Shahrani, Mohamed Al-Deaya

Past masters: Sayeed Al-Owairan, Al Bishi, Majed Mohammed

Denmark

Group C

Founded: 1889

FIFA: 1904

Despite being highly-ranked, Denmark have only reached the World Cup finals once before, in 1986, when they beat West Germany, Uruguay and Scotland to make the last 16 before losing to Spain. But they beat the best sides in Europe to win the European Championship in 1992 and have continued to produce players of great skill such as the Laudrup brothers – Brian and Michael – and goalkeeper Peter Schmeichel, rated as perhaps the best in the world.

Previous best in World Cup: Reached last 16 in 1986

Other honours: European Championship winners 1992, Olympic winners 1906

Coach: Bo Johansson

Star players: Peter Schmeichel, Brian Laudrup, Allan Nielsen

Past masters: Preben Elkjaer, Morten Olsen, Allan Simonsen

Spain

Group D

The Spanish team are proud to be attending another World Cup

Founded: 1913

FIFA: 1904

Spain are one of the great under-achievers in world football. Despite qualifying for the finals stages in nine out of 15 World Cups, Spain have never done better than finishing fourth in 1950. But they have a strong side that have grown out of the 1992 Olympic winners, and are expected to do well in France. Players such as Raul and Ivan de La Pena are rising stars to watch.

Previous best in World Cup: Fourth place in 1950

Other honours: European Champions in 1964, runners-up in 1984. Olympic Gold in 1992

Coach: Javier Clemente

Star players: Raul, Hierro, Miguel Angel Nadal

Past masters: Alfredo Di Stefano, Andoni Zubizarreta, Emilio Butragueno

Nigeria

Group D

Founded: 1945

FIFA: 1959

The "Green Eagles" of Nigeria made a major impact in their first World Cup finals appearance, at USA '94. They beat Bulgaria and Greece, and took Italy to extra time in their second round game before losing 2–1. They won the African Nations Cup that same year and took the Olympic title in 1996, beating Brazil in the final, to prove how good they are.

Celestine Babayaro jumps during a World Cup qualifier

Previous best in World Cup: Reached second round in 1994

Other honours: African Nations Cup winners in 1980 and 1994, Olympic Games Gold 1996

Coach: Vellbor "Bora" Milutinovic

Star players: Daniel Amokachi, Celestine Babayaro, Finidi George

Past masters: Stephen Keshi

Paraguay

Group D

The team celebrate a 1–1 draw at home to Argentina

Founded: 1906

FIFA: 1921

Paraguay have never progressed beyond the second round in their four finals appearances but have high hopes of getting to the quarter-finals at least under coach Paolo Cesar Carpeggiani, who played for Brazil in the 1970s and was a successful coach with Brazilian club side Flamengo. Goalkeeper Jose Luis Chilavert is a colourful character who has been known to take penalties and free-kicks!

Previous best in World Cup: Reached second round 1986

Other honours: Copa America winners in 1953 and 1979, runners-up 1929, 1947, 1949, 1963

Coach: Paolo Cesar Carpeggiani

Star players: Jose Luis Chilavert, Benitez, Gamarra

Past masters: Romerito, Arsenio Erico

Bulgaria

Group D

Founded: 1923

FIFA: 1924

This is only the third World Cup finals appearance for Bulgaria, who were the surprise package of USA '94. After a heavy defeat by Nigeria, they went on to beat Argentina, Mexico and then Germany in the quarter-finals before losing to Italy in the semi-finals. Hristo Stoichkov is their temperamental star player and was joint top scorer in the 1994 finals. Coach Hristo Bonev was the greatest goalscorer in Bulgaria's history.

Previous best in World Cup: 4th place in 1994

Other honours: European Championship quarter-finalists in 1968, Olympic runners-up 1968

Coach: Hristo Bonev

Star players: Hristo Stoichkov, Yordan Lechkov, Emil Kostadinov

Past masters: Hristo Bonev, Georgi Asparoukhov, Dmitr Penev

Holland

Group E

Founded:
1889

FIFA: 1904

Holland are the most unpredictable of the major footballing powers. Capable of producing superb teams and players, they have reached two World Cup finals and won the European Championship, but often they do not live up to their potential in major tournaments. Their first golden period was in the 1970s, when Ajax Amsterdam ruled Europe and the national side were considered the best in the world. In the 1980s Gullit, Van Basten and Frank Rijkaard reigned supreme, and now the Dutch have another group of highly talented players.

Bergkamp celebrates with Numan

Previous best in World Cup: Runners-up 1974 and 1978

Other honours: European Championship winners 1988

Coach: Guus Hiddink

Star players: Dennis Bergkamp, Partick Kluivert, Clarence Seedorf

Past masters: Johan Cruyff, Ruud Gullit, Marco Van Basten

Belgium

Group E

Founded:
1895

FIFA: 1904

The Belgians qualified, via the play-offs, for their fifth successive World Cup, by beating the Republic of Ireland 2–1 at home after a 1–1 draw in Dublin. Their current side is not as strong as the impressive side which reached the European Championship final in 1980, but they have one of Europe's deadliest strikers in Luc Nilis and a good record in major tournaments.

Luis Oliveira playing for Belgium in March 1997, in a game that they lost 3–1 to Holland

Previous best in World Cup: Reached semi-finals in 1986

Other honours: Olympic Champions 1920, European Championship runners-up 1980

Coach: Georges Leekens

Star players: Luc Nilis, Luis Oliveira, Frankie Van Der Elst

Past masters: Jean-Marie Pfaff, Eric Gerets, Jan Ceulemans

South Korea

Group E

Yoo Sang Chul will hope to play in the 2002 finals in South Korea, as well as in France in 1998

Founded: 1928

FIFA: 1948

South Korea are the strongest Asian team of recent years but they have never gone beyond the first round in four attempts so far. Now under the guidance of former star player Cha Bum Kun, who played in Germany for Bayer Leverkusen and Eintracht Frankfurt, the Koreans hope to reach the second round for the first time in their history. They will also be looking to perform well and justify FIFA's decision to make them co-hosts with Japan for the 2002 World Cup.

Previous best in World Cup: Never gone beyond first round

Other honours: Asian Champions in 1956 and 1960

Coach: Cha Bum Kun

Star players: Yoo Sang Chul, Bo Hong, Choi Yong Soo

Past masters: Choi Jeong Ming, Cha Bum Kun, Hong Myung Bo

Mexico

Group E

Founded: 1927

FIFA: 1929

Mexico have a strong record of qualifying for the World Cup, having reached the finals 10 times, and they hope to go better than 1994, when they lost on penalties to Bulgaria in the second round. Though they have lost experienced coach Bora Milutinovic, Manuel Lapuente will be hoping to emulate the Serb's 1986 feat of taking Mexico to the quarter-finals.

Previous best in World Cup: Quarter-finals in 1986

Other honours: CONCACAF champions in 1963, 1971, 1977, 1993. Copa America runners-up in 1993

Coach: Manuel Lapuente

Star players: Jorge Campos, Luis Suarez, Luis Garcia Aspe

Past masters: Antonio Carbajal, Hugo Sanchez, Luis Garcia

Germany

Group F

Founded: 1900

FIFA: 1904–1946, 1950

Germany are the most successful side in Europe and are among the favourites because of their phenomenal tournament record. They have reached 10 major finals, winning six of them, and have reached every World Cup since 1954. The current European Champions, they look to captain Klinsmann for goals and sweeper Sammer – 1996's European Footballer of the Year – for creativity. Coach Berti Vogts won a winner's medal in 1974 and was assistant coach in their 1990 success.

Previous best in World Cup: Winners 1954, 1974 and 1990, runners-up 1966 and 1986

Other honours: European Championship winners 1972, 1980, 1996, runners-up 1976 and 1992

Coach: Berti Vogts

Star players: Jürgen Klinsmann, Andreas Möller, Matthias Sammer

Past masters: Franz Beckenbauer, Gerd Müller, Lothar Matthäus

USA

Group F

Founded: 1913

FIFA: 1913

The USA have reached their third successive finals, having had a 40-year gap since taking part in the early tournaments. Football in the United States has risen again after their professional league collapsed in the 1970s, and the new Major League Soccer was given a big boost by the country's performance in 1994 when they were hosts to the World Cup. Although some players are based abroad, most of the squad have returned to play in the MSL.

Previous best in World Cup: Semi-final in 1930

Other honours: CONCACAF champions 1991, Copa America semi-finals 1995

Coach: Steve Sampson

Star players: Kasey Keller, John Harkes, Roy Wegerle

Past master: Larry Gaetjens

Yugoslavia

Group F

©1995 ISL TM

Yugoslavia were delighted to qualify for France '98 with a 12–1 aggregate win over Hungary

Founded: 1919

FIFA: 1919

Yugoslavia finished second in their qualifying group, behind Spain, yet they cruised through their play-off match with a 12–1 aggregate score over Hungary. Known as the Brazil of Europe for their skilful players, this is their first appearance in the final stages of a tournament since the 1990 World Cup. They were then banned from international competition between 1992 and 1994 because of civil war but are back as a strong force in European football once again.

Previous best in World Cup: Semi-finalists 1930 and 1962

Other honours: Olympic Champions 1960

Coach: Slobodan Santrac

Star players: Dejan Savicevic, Predrag Mijatovic, Savo Milosevic

Past masters: Ivan Bek, Dragan Dzajic, Dragoslav Sekularac

Iran

Group F

Founded: 1920

FIFA: 1948

Iran won the final place in France by beating Australia in the Asia/Oceania play-off, scoring twice in three minutes to gain a 2–2 draw in the second leg to go through on away goals. Iran's only previous appearance in the finals was in 1978, when they drew with Scotland but went out in the first round.

Brazilian coach Valdeir Vierra was in charge to see them past Australia but was replaced by Tomislav Ivic in January 1998. Striker Karim Bagheri scored seven times in an early qualifier against the Maldives.

Previous best in World Cup: Never gone beyond first round

Other honours: Asian Cup winners 1968, 1972 and 1976

Coach: Tomislav Ivic

Star players: Khodadad Azizi, Karim Bagheri, Ali Daei

Past masters: Danaie-Fard, Eskandarian

Romania

Group G

Founded: 1908

FIFA: 1930

Romania played some of the best football of the past two World Cups, in Italy and the USA, but failed to progress beyond the quarter-finals, losing on penalties both times. Midfield playmaker Gheorghe Hagi is one of the most talented players in world football when he is in top form, but he was disappointing at Euro '96 when Romania lost all three of their games. A lot depends on how he performs in France.

Previous best in World Cup: Quarter-finalists in 1990 and 1994

Other honours: European Championship – First round in 1984 and 1996

Coach: Anghel Iordanescu

Star players: Gica Popescu, Dan Petrescu, Gheorghe Hagi

Past masters: Ilie Dumitrescu, Rodion Camataru

Colombia

Group G

Founded: 1924

FIFA: 1936

Colombia have only recently emerged as a force in world football after years of internal and international problems. The country played no international football at all between 1949 and 1957 but managed to qualify for the 1962 World Cup. More recently they were expected to do well at the 1990 and 94 finals but were disappointing, despite having undoubted stars such as Valderrama, Asprilla and Rincon.

Previous best in World Cup: Reached last 16 in 1994

Other honours: Copa America runners-up in 1975

Coach: Hernan Dario Gomez

Star players: Faustino Asprilla, Freddy Rincon, Carlos Valderrama

Past masters: Rene Higuita, Wilson Perez, Andreas Escobar

England

Group G

Founded: 1863

FIFA: 1905–20, 1924–28, 1946

England are hoping for a successful return to France after winning Le Tournoi there last summer, ahead of Brazil, Italy and the French. The founders of modern football did not enter the World Cup until 1950 but won it as hosts in 1966. They went close in 1970 and 1990, but failed to qualify for USA '94. Since then they have emerged as a world power once again, with Alan Shearer one of the best strikers in the world when fit.

Previous best in World Cup: Winners 1966

Other honours: European Championship semi-finalists 1968 and 1996, Olympic winners 1908 and 1912

Coach: Glenn Hoddle

Star players: Paul Gascoigne, Paul Ince, Alan Shearer

Past masters: Bobby Moore, Bobby Charlton, Gary Lineker

Tunisia

Group G

Founded: 1956

FIFA: 1960

Tunisia's only previous appearance in the World Cup was in 1978 in Argentina, where they were unlucky not to reach the second round. In their three group matches they beat Mexico, which made them the first African side to win a match in the World Cup finals. They also held reigning champions West Germany to a goalless draw before losing to a Poland side which contained their current coach Henryk Kasperczak.

Previous best in World Cup: Never gone beyond first round

Other honours: African Nations Cup runners-up 1965

Coach: Henryk Kasperczak

Star players: Adel Sellimi, Samir Trabelsi, Ben Slimane

Past masters: Chetali

Argentina

Group H

Founded: 1893

FIFA: 1912

Argentina have participated in 10 previous World Cups and won the trophy twice, in 1978 when they were hosts and in 1986 in Mexico. They have also won the Copa America 14 times and after Brazil are the most powerful football nation outside Europe. Despite losing Diego Maradona, their star of the past decade, they are still a powerful side and are coached by Daniel Passarella, who captained the team that won the 1978 World Cup.

Previous best in World Cup: Winners 1978 and 1986, runners-up 1990

Other honours: Copa America champions 14 times

Coach: Daniel Passarella

Star players: Diego Simeone, Gabriel Batistuta, Ariel Ortega

Past masters: Diego Maradona, Osvaldo Ardiles, Mario Kempes

Japan

Group H

Founded: 1921

FIFA: 1929–45, 1950

This is Japan's first appearance at the finals following the sudden growth of football in the country, which only launched a professional league five years ago. The Japanese, who will co-host the 2002 finals with South Korea, changed managers during the qualifying stages, with Takeshi Okada taking over to steer them through a play-off victory over Iran that was secured by a "golden goal" in sudden death extra time.

Previous best in World Cup: First appearance

Other honours: Asian Cup winners 1992

Coach: Takeshi Okada

Star players: Hidetoshi Nakata, Tsuyoshi Kitazawa, Wagner Lopes

Past masters: Kazuyoshi Miura, Takuya Takagi and Masashi Nakayama

Jamaica

Group H

Founded: 1910

FIFA: 1962

Jamaica are only the second Caribbean country to reach the finals, after Haiti did so in 1974. The Reggae Boyz, as they are nicknamed, held Mexico to a 0–0 draw in their twentieth and last qualifying game, and thereby finished behind the USA in their CONCACAF group. Brazilian coach Rene Simoes has recruited a number of English Premiership stars with Jamaican backgrounds for his squad.

Previous best in World Cup: First appearance

Other honours: none

Coach: Rene Simoes

Star players: Deon Burton, Robbie Earle, Paul Hall

Croatia

Group H

Founded: 1991

FIFA: 1992

For a relatively young footballing nation Croatia have made a big impact. After leading the scoring during the European Championship qualifying games, the Croatian team did not live up to expectations in the finals. Their World Cup qualifying progress was equally disappointing in a group which they should have won. They eventually qualified after a play-off against Ukraine, but they do have enough talented players to beat most countries on their day.

Previous best in World Cup: First appearance

Other honours: Reached quarter-finals of Euro 96

Coach: Miroslav Blazevic

Star players: Slaven Bilic, Aljosa Asanovic, Davor Suker, Zvonimir Boban, Robert Prosinecki, Alen Boksic

© 1974 FIFA TM

The Results

Once the World Cup begins, you can use the tables to help you follow the progress of all the teams. Fill in the tables on these pages once all first round matches are complete, by checking the results on TV or in your newspaper. Then fill in the gaps on pages 62 and 63 of this book as the action unfolds.

© 1974 FIFA TM

First Round

Group A – Final Table

Brazil • Scotland • Morocco • Norway

Team	Played	Won	Drawn	Lost	For	Against	Points
1							
2							
3							
4							

Group B – Final Table

Italy • Chile • Cameroon • Austria

Team	Played	Won	Drawn	Lost	For	Against	Points
1							
2							
3							
4							

Group C – Final Table

France • South Africa • Saudi Arabia • Denmark

Team	Played	Won	Drawn	Lost	For	Against	Points
1							
2							
3							
4							

Group D – Final Table

Spain • Nigeria • Paraguay • Bulgaria

Team	Played	Won	Drawn	Lost	For	Against	Points
1							
2							
3							
4							

Group E – Final Table

Holland • Belgium • South Korea • Mexico

Team	Played	Won	Drawn	Lost	For	Against	Points
1							
2							
3							
4							

Group F – Final Table

Germany • United States • Yugoslavia • Iran

Team	Played	Won	Drawn	Lost	For	Against	Points
1							
2							
3							
4							

Group G – Final Table

Romania • Colombia • England • Tunisia

Team	Played	Won	Drawn	Lost	For	Against	Points
1							
2							
3							
4							

Group H – Final Table

Argentina • Japan • Jamaica • Croatia

Team	Played	Won	Drawn	Lost	For	Against	Points
1							
2							
3							
4							

Second Round

Game 1 – June 27: Paris

.... vs ....
Winner of group A — Runner up of group B

Game 2 – June 27: Marseille

.... vs ....
Winner of group B — Runner up of group A

Game 3 – June 28: Lens

.... vs ....
Winner of group C — Runner up of group D

Game 4 – June 28: St Denis

.... vs ....
Winner of group D — Runner up of group C

Game 5 – June 29: Toulouse

.... vs ....
Winner of group E — Runner up of group F

Game 6 – June 29: Montpellier

.... vs ....
Winner of group F — Runner up of group E

Game 7 – June 30: Bordeaux

.... vs ....
Winner of group G — Runner up of group H

Game 8 – June 30: St Etienne

.... vs ....
Winner of group H — Runner up of group G